F.A.B.

Fake
Ain't
Beautiful

Once upon a time, there was a young African American girl name Izzie. Izzie was your average girl from next door. Everybody knew Izzie and the one thing everybody knew about Izzie was that she loved her family, friends, but most importantly Izzie loved her hair. Yes, her hair.

Why her hair? Because it was bouncy like a ball and it was full like a lion's mane. Izzie loved her hair so much that every morning, she would have to get up one hour early just to make sure her hair was together for the next morning.

Izzie had to get up extra early every morning just to do her hair. It was so bad that her sister Rhonni would have to bang on the bathroom door and scream "Izzie hurry up I have to use the bathroom". Rhonni did not have big full hair like her sister. Rhonni's hair was short and curly. Rhonni preferred short hair over long hair because she would get tired of getting a perm and her hair would poof right back into her afro. Rhonni cut her hair almost 3 years ago, once she realized that long hair was just not working out for her.

Rhonni tried to get Izzie to cut her hair almost 2 years ago but she did not want to cut her hair because she knew that she felt beautiful with her hair. Izzie told Rhonni "I am not cutting my hair; my hair is what makes me feel beautiful".

Izzie was in high school and she was a part of everything. When I say everything, I do mean everything. Izzie was so popular that the security guard knew who Izzie was by name and by face but of course Izzie's hair.

Izzie's best friend Lashun met her at their locker because they shared lockers and Lashun made sure that Izzie had some snacks because they would eat in class together because that's just how much they loved food and lunch was not getting there fast enough for them.

Everybody knew Lashun and Izzie were best friend because they were always together, and they were inseparable. Lashun had so many hair styles. She had a different hair style every week. She was a total diva. But that's what Izzie admired about her the most.

She did not care about what people thought about her or her hair.

While at school, teachers and some students would ask Izzie what do she do to keep her hair maintain?

She would tell them the full story about how she would have to get up every morning an hour early and use her favorite hair products. Her favorite products were Cantu or Cream of Nature. But the only thing Izzie did not like was when she ran out. Nature Hair products were not cheap! Izzie did not let anybody use her products because one bottle of Cream of Nature was fifteen dollars. Nature hair products were not cheap at all. That's why Izzie left her products at home and did not carry them around with her.

Izzie's favorite teacher in school was Mrs. Jalisa West. She was so confident in everything she did. The way she dressed was just unique but always professional. Everybody loved Mrs. West. She could put any color any pattern together and it would just be cute. Izzie and Mrs. West had so much in common, the only thing is Mrs. West had short blonde hair and Izzie had big black hair. But every day they would talk about how Izzie should try cutting her hair, because Izzie would complain about how her hair would take up so much of her time in the morning.

And some people were complaining in class how they couldn't see because of how big Izzie's hair was.
Izzie felt bad because sometimes she would do her hair and she did not like it, but she knew everybody else loved her hair. She would sit in her room and look at different people with short hair styles and just

think to herself how she would look with short hair.

Izzie felt as if she would look ugly with short hair or people would judge her because of the idea of having short hair.

Izzie went and talk to her parents Denise and Devon.

Devon, Izzie's father told her that he would love the fact that if she cut her hair, she would not be FAKE.

He meant that you are beautiful without weave and you are beautiful with or without hair. Hair does not define you.

Izzie's mother though it was not a bad idea because Izzie's mother was getting tired of spending all the money on Izzie's hair and it was going right back into an Afro. Denise though it was not such a bad idea that she even though about cutting her hair too. Izzie showed them what styles she was thinking about cutting her hair like, but she was not ready to cut it just yet. She needed some more opinions. Izzie called her best friend to get her opinion on Izzie cutting her hair. Izzie did not beat around the bush to tell Lashun about cutting her hair. But Izzie did not know how Lashun was going to respond when she told her that she wanted to cut her hair.

Lashun told Izzie that she would love it no matter if Izzie cut her hair or not. It was up to her.

Lashun was her go to person when she needed

a second opinion. Izzie though long and hard about it but she still needed

another opinion. Izzie stayed up half of the night talking to her best friend and on google looking at different styles and cuts because Izzie knew she wanted to cut her hair but she was scared because she thought she would be ugly and would not feel so confident without her hair. But Izzie

remembered what her father had told her. "You are not FAKE".

Izzie was having a bad hair day at school because she had overslept and did not get up on time to do her hair. Days like this Izzie wanted to cut her hair because if she did, it would be simple as get

up, brush your hair down, and walk out the door. Izzie still needed one more opinion about cutting her hair. After today's bad hair day. Izzie wanted to cut it all off.

It was lunch time and Izzie told Lashun she would meet her in the cafeteria. Izzie went to Mrs. West classroom to go talk to her. Mrs. West was eating lunch but she told Izzie to come in so they could talk.

Mrs. West could tell Izzie had something on her mind because she was not as bubbly as she was on a normal day. Izzie had explained to Mrs. West that she was having a bad hair day and she had to grab a beanie and make it work for today until she got home. That normal routine played a big part in Izzie's life. Not doing Izzie's hair is like not putting sugar in your coffee. Lunch time was over, and Mrs. West was getting ready for her next class to come in and Izzie had to go to class herself. One more period and school was almost over for the day. Izzie couldn't wait to go home and call Jennie. Jennie was Izzie's big sister. They treated each other like family for many years. They know each other since they were six years old.

So, Jennie was more family than anything. Jennie was much older than Izzie was. But they lived on two opposite ends of the city ever since Jennie moved when they were about 14 years old. But that did not stop them from hanging with each other over the weekend. Jennie was the fashionista; she changed her hair like she changed her bra. Every week it was something different. Now Jennie did weave all the time. But no matter what she did, Jennie was always there for Izzie when she needed her advice about her hair.

After school, Jennie came and picked Izzie up from school. Jennie saw that Izzie had a bad hair day because of the beanie she had on. They went out for coffee at Starbucks and they talked about each other's day at school. Izzie and Jennie went to two different high schools.

Izzie wanted to go to the same school as Jennie did, but her mom was not having it.

It was in a different school district and Izzie mom wasn't going that far from the house just to take us to school.

Jennie told Izzie that she would help get her hair together so she wouldn't have to do it in the morning. They pulled up to Izzie's house and walked in the house. Devon was on the computer working as usual and Rhonni was upstairs on her game. Denise hadn't made it home yet from work. Jennie spoke to Devon and Devon spoke back. They went upstairs to Izzie room so Izzie could tell Jennie that she was ready for the big chop, but she was afraid that she would look ugly and wouldn't feel the same as she did with her hair. Jennie begun to do Izzie hair while Izzie was on Pinterest strolling through the different short natural hair styles.

They talked and laugh, and Izzie realized she kept putting the conversation off. So, Jeannie finally said it, "What's wrong Izz, you

been bummed out about this hair thing all evening". Izzie could not keep her problems to herself. Her dad always said, "I can tell when something is wrong with you before you even knock on the door, it's all over your face".

Izzie tried so hard to always keep her problems to herself, but it never worked. Izzie finally told Jennie the truth. "Jennie, I want to cut my hair off" Izzie said. "Ok, what's the issue" Jennie said. "I'm afraid that people will not like me because my hair is gone, and I won't feel beautiful without my hair." "People will judge me and call me a little boy if I cut it off".

"What if I cut it and I don't have the natural look"?

Jennie looked at Izzie with a confused look because she was trying to understand what the natural look was. Plus, Jennie was trying to understand what her baby sister was talking about when she said she was not beautiful without her hair. Izzie looked at Jennie and said, "Why you keep looking at me like that"? Jennie sat face to face with Izzie and told her "Izzie don't you ever say that you are not beautiful. Because that is the biggest lie you can ever tell yourself." "

Never let a soul tell you that" Izzie started to feel her confidence go back up because of what her sister had told her.

Izzie knew
Then it was time to make
The big chop.
Rhonni over-heard the conversation that Jennie and Izzie were having, and she came into Izzie room and said "Well, praise the lord, it's about time you finally coming to your senses about your hair. Cut it off girl it can grow back if you really wanted it too."

Izzie smiled at Rhonni and Jennie and gave

Jennie a hug. Izzie needed that one opinion to confirm that she was going to do the big chop. Jennie left so she could get home at a decent time and Izzie went downstairs to tell her mom and dad that it was time and she was ready.

Izzie went to the family barber right around the corner from their house. She told Arthur that she was ready for the big chop and she wanted a short natural afro.

Izzie's hair had a curl pattern to it. The moment it got wet, it was short curly and in a fro. Izzie was confident about this cut. She wasn't nervous or anything.

She could own it.

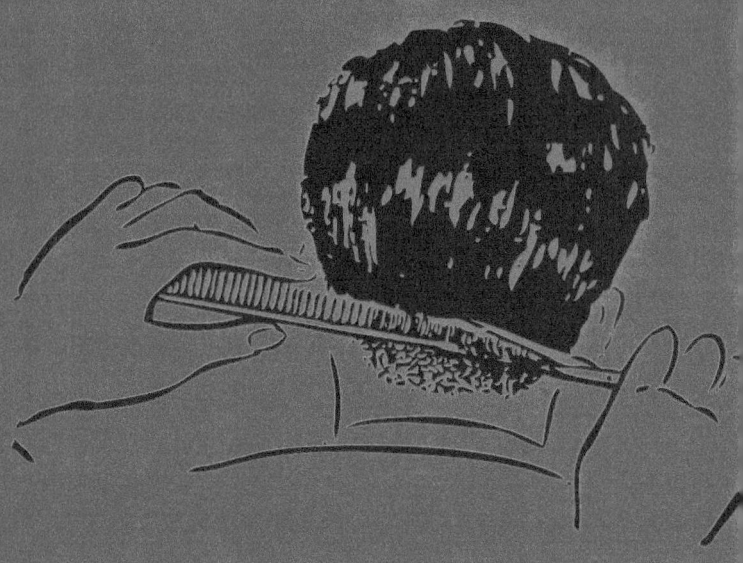

Izzie woke up the next morning getting ready to start her daily routine, when she went into the bathroom, her hair was gone.

No more getting up extra early just to fool with her hair. It was as simple as one two three. Moisturizer, a head band and walk out the door. Izzie had the biggest smile on her face, you could see all 32 teeth. Rhonni was just about to bang on the bathroom door, but before she could even do that, Izzie opened the door and said, "It's all yours now, I'm done now". Rhonni looked at Izzie and just started smiling.

Denise and Devon saw Izzie and they smiled at her because they knew how happy Izzie felt about her new hair style and they could tell that Izzie was having a great morning. Denise told Izzie that she really liked her hair cut and she didn't think Izzie would cut it that short, but she did. Devon loved it all together and all Devon kept saying was "Fake Ain't Beautiful Izzie" Izzie smiled and was ready for school. Mainly she was ready to see what everybody was reaction going to be once they saw that she had did the big chop. Most importantly Izzie was ready to see what her best friend was going to say when she saw her this morning at school.

Izzie and Rhonni got dropped off at school and Izzie could tell that everybody was shocked just by the way they were looking at her. Izzie didn't care if anybody had anything negative to say.

Lashun finally saw Izzie and screamed "OMG YOU DID IT!"

"Izzie smiled and said, "Yeah bestie I did it" Students were coming up to Izzie telling her that her haircut looked very nice on her and that it fit her. Izzie was enjoying all the attention and compliments. Lashun was ready to take pictures with Izzie and get on Snap Chat. Izzie was just smiling from ear to ear. Mrs. West saw Izzie in the hallway, and she gave her that look like "Yes ,Ma'am, honey you better work it and own it" ! Izzie gave Mrs. West a hug and told her thank you for all their talks about cutting her hair.

Izzie realized that with or without hair you are still beautiful. Weave does not determine your sense of beauty or confidence. Weave is not made for everybody, but it works for some people and others feel as though the natural look works for them.

In this case, the natural look worked for Izzie. Ever since the big chop happen, Izzie has never thought about growing her hair ever again. She loves to keep it short and curly and off her back. Izzie will never forget all the positive feedback she got, and she will never forget her father's words.

"Fake Ain't Beautiful"

Eboni Johnson is a 2018 Rust College Graduate majored in Mass Communications -Print Journalism. Eboni started this writing journey when she was just a sophomore in high school. She has her own publishing company *Extravagant Publications, LLC* .

It has been in business for 1year now and she enjoys every minute of it. Eboni plans to further her career in Journalism and continue to write and publish more works later in life.

Dedication Page
I would like to dedicate my first book to my family who supported me through this process. Also I would like to say thank you the ladies of Zeta Phi Beta Iota Gamma Chapter for love and support.

www.ingramcontent.com/pod-product-compliance
Lightning Source LLC
Chambersburg PA
CBHW040302010526
44108CB00033B/20